SCIENCE SLEUTHS

?

PREDICT IT!

Monday	Tuesday	Wednesday	Thursday
			Prediction

AZZA SHARKAWY

Crabtree Publishing Company

www.crabtreebooks.com

D1070377

SCIENCE SLEUTHS

?

Author
Azza Sharkawy

Publishing plan research and development
Reagan Miller

Editors
Shirley Duke, Reagan Miller, Kathy Middleton

Proofreader and indexer
Wendy Scavuzzo

Photo research
Katherine Berti

Design
Katherine Berti

Print and production coordinator
Katherine Berti

Photographs and illustrations
Getty Images: Leslie Miller: p.14
istock: p. 20
Thinkstock: p. 8 (bottom left); p. 17; p21

All other images by Shutterstock

Library and Archives Canada Cataloguing in Publication

Sharkawy, Azza, author
        Predict it! / Azza Sharkawy.

(Science sleuths)
Includes index.
Issued in print and electronic formats.
ISBN 978-0-7787-0773-8 (bound).--ISBN 978-0-7787-0796-7 (pbk.).--
ISBN 978-1-4271-7713-1 (pdf).--ISBN 978-1-4271-7707-0 (html)

        1. Weather forecasting--Juvenile literature. 2. Pattern
perception--Juvenile literature. I. Title.

QC995.43S43 2014   j551.63   C2014-903940-9
                                                                      C2014-903941-7

Library of Congress Cataloging-in-Publication Data

Sharkawy, Azza, author.
 Predict it! / Azza Sharkawy.
      pages cm. -- (Science sleuths)
 Includes index.
 ISBN 978-0-7787-0773-8 (reinforced library binding) -- ISBN 978-0-7787-0796-7
(pbk.) -- ISBN 978-1-4271-7713-1 (electronic pdf) -- ISBN 978-1-4271-7707-0
(electronic html)
1. Observation (Scientific method)--Juvenile literature. 2. Science--
Methodology--Juvenile literature. 3. Weather forecasting--Juvenile literature.
I. Title.

 Q175.2.S529 2015
 507.2'1--dc23
                                          2014032324

Crabtree Publishing Company

www.crabtreebooks.com   1-800-387-7650

Printed in Canada/102014/EF20140925

Published in Canada
Crabtree Publishing
616 Welland Ave.
St. Catharines, Ontario
L2M 5V6

Published in the United States
Crabtree Publishing
PMB 59051
350 Fifth Avenue, 59th Floor
New York, New York 10118

Published in the United Kingdom
Crabtree Publishing
Maritime House
Basin Road North, Hove
BN41 1WR

Published in Australia
Crabtree Publishing
3 Charles Street
Coburg North
VIC 3058

CONTENTS

WHAT WILL HAPPEN?

You wake up in the morning and see the ground is covered in snow. You get dressed and go out. The snow is up to your knees. The last time it was that deep, school was canceled. You're sure that today will be a "snow day!"

You didn't just make a lucky guess.
You were thinking like a scientist!

The natural world includes **living** and **non-living** things, such as people, plants, rocks, and water.

Scientists **predict**, or make guesses about what might happen in the future based on what they know now.

How do scientists learn new facts about the **natural world**? The same way you do. They **observe**, or gather information by using their five senses: sight, hearing, taste, smell, and touch.

FINDING PATTERNS

How do scientists make **predictions**? They start by observing and gathering new information. They also use facts they learned in the past.

They use this information to look for **patterns**. A pattern is something that repeats over and over. Patterns help scientists make sense of information.

Bees build a honeycomb using one six-sided shape over and over.

Patterns are everywhere in nature. There are many different kinds of patterns. We can see patterns in shapes and in sounds. Patterns can also be a set of changes that happen in an order. For example, all people start out as babies. As they grow, they change into a child, then a teenager, and finally an adult.

PATTERNS IN NATURE

What patterns do you notice when you look at nature? Night always comes after day. You have seen this pattern repeat itself every day. Each morning, the sun appears to rise in one part of the sky. It moves across the sky, then sets on the other side. The sun does the same thing again the next day.

sunrise

midday

sunset

At nighttime, we can see part of the moon lit up in the sky. The shape we see changes a bit each day. Sometimes the moon looks round. Sometimes it's just a sliver. The moon goes through the same set of shapes every 28 days.

EXPLORE IT!

?

Observe the moon and draw its shape every night for 28 days. On day 29, draw what you think the moon's shape will be before you look up in the sky. Were you right?

We can't see the shape called a new moon from Earth, but it is still part of the moon's 28-day pattern.

Sunday	Monday	Tuesday	Wednesday	Thursday	Friday	Saturday
1	2	3	4	5	6	7
8	9	10	11	12	13	14
15	16	17	18	19	20	21
22	23	24	25	26	27	28 New Moon
29	30					

9

PATTERNS IN SEASONS

How many times have you seen each season since you were born? You have observed the four seasons come in the same order every year—winter, spring, summer, and fall. They follow a pattern that repeats. You can predict that fall will come after summer next year, too.

If a pattern has repeated in the past, it will probably continue to repeat in the future. Observing patterns helps scientists predict what will happen in the future.

Do you change during the seasons? Think about the activities you do and the clothes you wear. Can you think of other changes?

EXPLORE IT!

?

Describe the pattern of changes that trees go through from season to season.

PREDICTING THE WEATHER

Meteorologists are scientists that observe the weather to predict what it will be like in the days ahead. One way they predict weather is by observing clouds. They look at the shape and color of the clouds, as well as how high up they are. They may see low, gray clouds that look flat. They have learned these kinds of clouds bring rain.

OBSERVING CLOUDS

Cumulus clouds are white and puffy like cotton balls. Small cumulus clouds are a sign of good weather.

Cirrus clouds are thin, wispy clouds that form very high in the sky. Cirrus clouds usually mean the weather is sunny. But they are also a sign that the weather will change.

Stratus clouds form lower in the sky. They usually cover the sky like a gray blanket. Stratus clouds are the ones that bring light rain or snow.

cumulus clouds

cirrus clouds

stratus clouds

EXPLORE IT!

This girl is carrying an umbrella based on the meteorologist's prediction. What kind of clouds do you think the meteorologist saw?

13

DAILY WEATHER

Meteorologists measure the weather by using tools. They measure **temperature** with a thermometer. Temperature is a measure of how hot or cold it is. Scientists measure temperature in degrees Celsius.

Scientists record, or write down, these measurements. They organize the information onto charts. Then they study the charts and **graphs** to look for patterns in the weather. Patterns help them predict, or forecast, what the weather will be like later on.

Daily temperature tracking chart

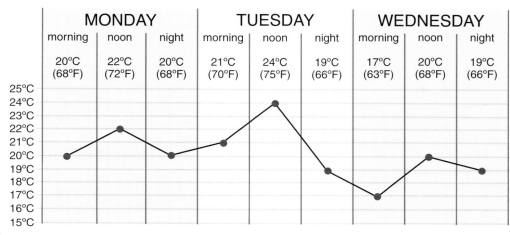

MONDAY			TUESDAY			WEDNESDAY		
morning	noon	night	morning	noon	night	morning	noon	night
20°C (68°F)	22°C (72°F)	20°C (68°F)	21°C (70°F)	24°C (75°F)	19°C (66°F)	17°C (63°F)	20°C (68°F)	19°C (66°F)

EXPLORE IT!

The line graph on this page shows temperatures at three different times of day. Which of the following patterns does the information show?

- It is warmer at night than it is at noon.

- It is cooler in the morning than it is at noon.

PATTERNS OVER TIME

Scientists also gather information for longer periods of time. For example, each season has its own usual weather patterns. Winter months usually have colder temperatures. Spring months usually have more rain.

Sunday	Monday	Tuesday	Wednesday	Thursday	Friday	Saturday
1	2	3	4	5	6	7
8	9	10	11	12	13	14
15	16	17	18	19	20	21
22	23	24	25	26	27	28
29	30					

This girl has recorded her **observations** of the weather each day for a month. She has counted up the number of sunny, cloudy, rainy, and snowy days. Using what you know about weather, what season do you think her information is describing?

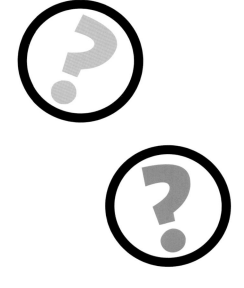

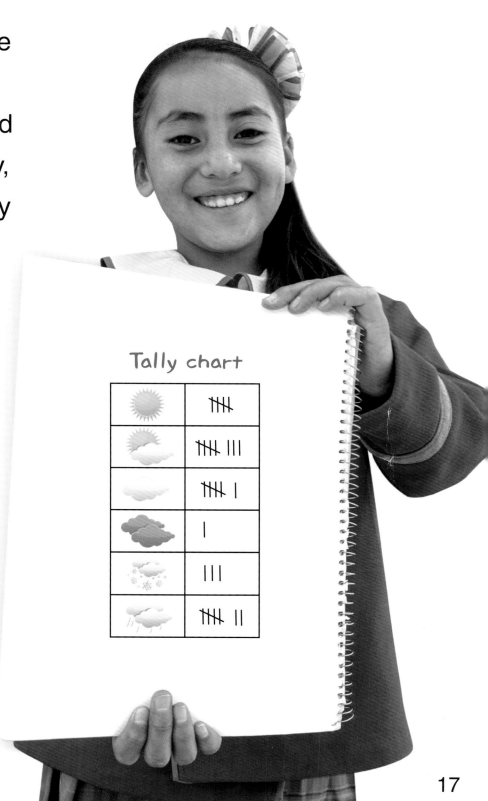

Tally chart

☀	卌
⛅	卌 III
☁	卌 I
☁	I
❄	III
🌧	卌 II

WEATHER WARNINGS

Weather **forecasts** help us do more than just choose the right clothes. Some weather can be unsafe. It can be dangerous to drive during an ice storm. It can also be unsafe to be outside when there is lightning.

Meteorologists help keep us safe. If they predict unsafe weather is coming, we can stay inside for protection. For example, a warning on TV can give people time to go somewhere safe if a **tornado** is predicted.

This meteorologist is warning people about powerful winds and rain from a **hurricane**.

EVERYDAY PREDICTIONS

You make predictions every day based on your own observations. You look outside the window to see what the weather will be like that day. You guess who stole the treasure in the story you are reading based on the clues.

Your school's basketball team has won every game so far this year. You predict they will win the championship!

WHAT DO YOU PREDICT?

You have learned that predictions are based on what you know. Read the sentences below. Think like a scientist and use what you know to predict what will happen next.

- The storm is getting worse. Lightning flashes across the sky. The lights in your house begin to flicker.

- The baseball game is about to begin. Everyone on the field is looking up at the sky. It's covered with low, gray clouds.

- Gus is over at his best friend's house. Their cat is very friendly. Gus loves cats, but he has an allergy to cat hair.

BASED ON FACTS

You have learned that predictions are based on what you know. Read the sentences below. Think like a scientist and figure out which predictions are based on facts.

- My dog will learn to talk.
- I will win an Olympic gold medal in tree climbing!
- We will eat turkey next Thanksgiving.
- My hair will turn purple tomorrow.
- I will be older on my next birthday.
- My younger brother will be older than me next year.

LEARNING MORE

BOOKS

Being a Scientist by Natalie Lunis and Nancy White. Newbridge Educational Publishing, 1999.

How do clouds form? by Lynn Peppas. Crabtree Publishing, 2012.

Weather Patterns by Monica Hughes. Heinemann, 2004.

WEBSITES

Learn how meteorologists predict the weather.
www.weatherwizkids.com/ weather-forecasting.htm

This video reviews what predictions are in science and how they are different from regular guesses.
www.youtube.com/ watch?v=hXQh0Fopd44

Play games, watch videos, and learn a lot about the weather.
http://pbskids.org/sid/ fablab_mainmenu.html

GLOSSARY

Note: Some boldfaced words are defined where they appear in the book.

forecasts (FOHR-kahsts) noun Predictions about the weather

graphs (GRAFZ) noun A diagram which shows measurements of things using lines or bars

hurricane (HUR-i-keyn) noun A very strong storm with strong wind and heavy rain

living (LIV-ing) adjective Alive; Plants and animals are examples of living things.

natural world (NACH-er-uhl WURLD) noun All living and non-living things in the world

non-living (non LIV-ing) adjective Not alive; Rocks and water are examples of non-living things.

observations (ob-zur-VEY-shuh nz) noun Facts you learn using your senses

observe (ob-ZURV) verb To gather information using your senses

patterns (PAT-ernz) noun Things that repeat over and over

predict (pri-DIKT) verb Using observations to tell what you think will happen next or in the future

predictions (pri-DIK-shuh nz) noun Things you have said will happen based on observations

temperature (TEM-per-uh-cher) noun The measure of how hot or cold something is

tornado (tawr-NEY-doh) noun A violent windstorm in a funnel shape that moves over land

An adjective is a word that describes what something is like.
A noun is a person, place, or thing.
A verb is an action word that tells you what someone or something does.

INDEX